TITANIC

Creating Titanic

The Ship of Dreams

by Kevin Blake

Consultant: Melinda E. Ratchford, EdD
Titanic Historian and Associate Professor
Sister Christine Beck Department of Education
Belmont Abbey College
Belmont, North Carolina

BEARPORT
PUBLISHING

New York, New York

Credits

Publisher: Kenn Goin
Senior Editor: Joyce Tavolacci
Creative Director: Spencer Brinker
Photo Research: Editorial Directions, Inc.

CENTRAL ARKANSAS LIBRARY SYSTEM
FLETCHER BRANCH LIBRARY
LITTLE ROCK, ARKANSAS

Library of Congress Cataloging-in-Publication Data

Names: Blake, Kevin, 1978– author.
Title: Creating titanic : the ship of dreams / by Kevin Blake ; consultant, Melinda E. Ratchford, EdD, Associate Professor, Sister Christine Beck Department of Education Belmont Abbey College, Belmont, North Carolina.
Description: New York, New York : Bearport Publishing, 2018. | Series: Titanica | Includes bibliographical references and index.
Identifiers: LCCN 2017034456 (print) | LCCN 2017049808 (ebook) | ISBN 9781684024889 (ebook) | ISBN 9781684024308 (library)
Subjects: LCSH: Titanic (Steamship)—Juvenile literature. | Shipbuilding—Juvenile literature.
Classification: LCC G530.T6 (ebook) | LCC G530.T6 B5938 2018 (print) | DDC 910.9163/4—dc23
LC record available at https://lccn.loc.gov/2017034456

For more information, write to Bearport Publishing Company, Inc., 45 West 21st Street, Suite 3B, New York, New York 10011. Printed in the United States of America.

10 9 8 7 6 5 4 3 2 1

CONTENTS

LAUNCHED!

On May 31, 1911, thousands of excited people crammed into a **shipyard** in Belfast, Ireland. They were there to watch the empty **hull** of RMS *Titanic* enter the water for the very first time. Brass bands played while dazzling red rockets exploded in the sky. Proud workers hugged their children as they pointed at the **massive** ship they had helped build.

The *Titanic* was 882.5 feet (269 m) long—almost as long as 3 football fields—and would be taller than a 10-story building. The ship weighed 46,328 tons (42,028 mt), or more than 8,000 elephants! Workers had covered the *Titanic* with 22 tons (20 mt) of soap, grease, and oil to help it slide out of its **berth** and into a sea **inlet**. In just 62 seconds, the giant **ocean liner** was floating for the very first time. It was the largest moving object the world had ever seen!

The *Titanic* slides into the water on launch day. It would be another ten months of work before the *Titanic* was completely finished and ready to set sail on her first trip.

Launch
OF
White Star Royal Mail Triple-Screw Steamer
"TITANIC"
At BELFAST,
Wednesday, 31st May, 1911, at 12-15 p.m.
Admit Bearer.

An invitation to the launch of the *Titanic*

The official name of the ship was the RMS *Titanic*. *RMS* stands for "Royal Mail Steamer." The *Titanic* received this name because it could carry mail and cargo from Great Britain around the world.

SEA RACE

Why had such a gigantic ship been built? In the early 1900s, before jet travel existed, the fastest way to cross the Atlantic Ocean was on a steamship. During that time, millions of **immigrants** looking for a better life boarded ships headed for America. A smaller number of wealthy people also traveled by ship for business or on **luxurious** vacations.

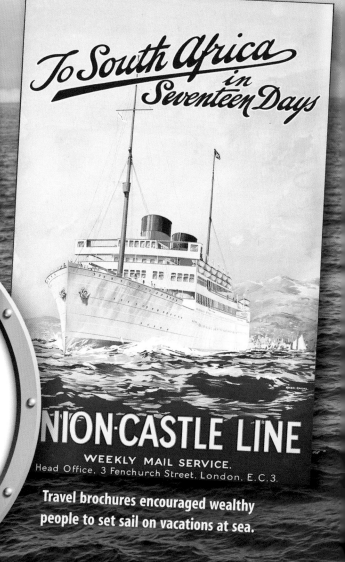

Travel brochures encouraged wealthy people to set sail on vacations at sea.

In the early 1900s, steamships had three categories of **passengers**. First-class passengers paid the most for their tickets and had the best accommodations. Second-class passengers had more basic rooms. Third-class, or **steerage**, passengers were housed below deck and had fewer **amenities**.

With the number of passengers increasing in the 1900s, there was a huge demand for bigger, faster, and fancier ships. In 1906, a shipping company called the Cunard Line built the fastest ocean liner in the world—the RMS *Lusitania*. How could any other shipping company compete with the *Lusitania*?

The *Lusitania* could carry passengers from Liverpool, England, to New York City in about five days.

A large crowd of European immigrants aboard an ocean liner

DREAMING BIG

J. Bruce Ismay, the chairman of the White Star Line, which was Cunard's biggest **rival**, had an exciting idea. He would construct the largest, most powerful ocean liner in the world. It would carry thousands of passengers and be so luxurious that wealthy people would feel as if they were traveling in a floating **mansion**. He would call his ship the *Titanic*.

The *Titanic* would be fast, too— crossing the ocean in six days.

J. Bruce Ismay

In 1907, Ismay met William Pirrie, the head of the Harland and Wolff shipbuilding company, for dinner at his London home. Over cigars and wine, Ismay shared his dream of an ocean liner so enormous and fancy that it would outshine the *Lusitania*. Pirrie loved the idea, and he knew the perfect **architect** to build the ship—his nephew, Thomas Andrews.

Harland and Wolff was one of the biggest and best shipbuilding companies in the world. The company, based in Belfast, Ireland, built all of White Star Line's ships.

William Pirrie

Harland and Wolff's offices

WHERE TO BUILD?

Thomas Andrews and his team soon went to work drawing up plans for the *Titanic*. However, there was a major problem. Where do you build such an enormous ship? The *Titanic* would be so big that it could not be constructed in a typical shipyard or with regular equipment.

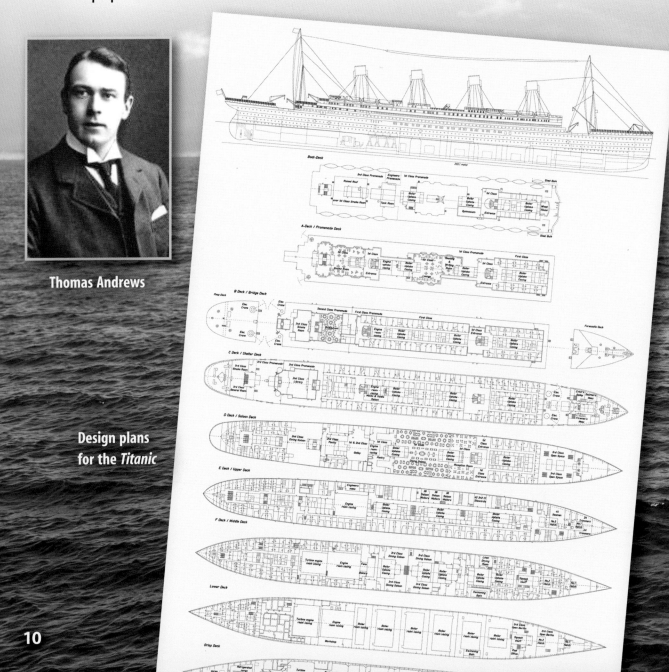

Thomas Andrews

Design plans for the *Titanic*

Andrews needed to think creatively to solve this problem. First, he ordered workers to demolish three **slipways**, or dry docks, at the Harland and Wolff shipyards. Then, the slipways were combined to make a large enough area to house the new ship. Andrews had a 220-foot (67 m) crane specially made so that workers would be able to reach the top of the vessel. Finally, he ordered a second crane from Germany that could lift 200 tons (181 mt). By March of 1909, it was time to start building the mighty *Titanic*.

Harland and Wolff would build two other gigantic ocean liners for the White Star Line at the same time as the *Titanic*. These were the *Olympic* and the *Britannic*. The *Titanic*—the largest of the three—was named after the Titans, who were ancient Greek gods.

The huge slipway at the Belfast shipyard

ARMY OF WORKERS

It would take an army of workers to construct the largest ship ever built. The team included thousands of carpenters, electricians, dockworkers, and **riveters**. All of the workers would be overseen by the *Titanic*'s general manager, Alexander Carlisle. Working on the ship would not only be difficult, it would also be dangerous—as the men quickly discovered.

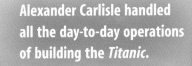

Alexander Carlisle handled all the day-to-day operations of building the *Titanic*.

Workers at the Belfast shipyard

The workers were given little protection from injury. At the time, there were no hardhats to keep workers' heads safe from falling objects. Nor was there any equipment to protect workers' ears from loud noises. The risk of falling was a constant threat. Despite these dangers, the men were proud of their work. *Titanic* worker Frank Parkinson came home every night to tell his family about the **majestic** ship he was building. His young son asked, "How can a ship that big stay up in the water?" Parkinson responded confidently, "That ship will always stay up."

In all, roughly 11,000 men worked together to build the *Titanic*. Nearly 250 men were seriously hurt, and, sadly, 8 people died building the ship.

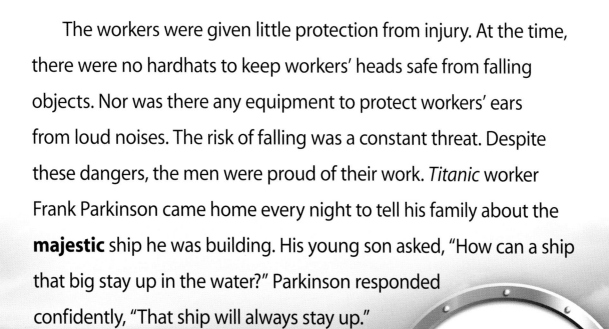

Workers stand next to the *Titanic*'s massive propellers.

THE SKELETON AND SKIN

During the first stage of construction, the workers built the ship's huge skeleton, or framework. The very first step was to lay down the ship's bottom, or **keel**. The keel worked like a giant backbone to hold the rest of the ship in place. Then they constructed a powerful steel frame—or hull—that stretched out from the backbone like ribs.

The *Titanic*'s hull (left) next to its sister ship the *Olympic*

The next task was to fasten 2,000 overlapping steel **plates** onto the skeleton that would serve as the ship's skin. Each plate was 6 feet (1.8 m) wide and 20 feet (6 m) long and weighed around 3 tons (2.7 mt). It took many hours of work and more than 3 million rivets—or small metal pins—to connect the skin to the ship's skeleton.

Each team of riveters had five members. Two people heated the rivet until it was red hot. Another person put it in the correct spot. Finally, two more men, called bashers, hammered the rivet into place.

A red-hot rivet

THE SHIP'S MUSCLES

A tremendous amount of force would be needed to power a ship as big as the *Titanic*. The ship's planners decided to use three steam-powered engines—each as tall as a six-story building! To create enough steam, 29 **boilers** would be used to super-heat nearly 400,000 gallons (1,514,165 l) of water. The steam would power the engines, allowing the *Titanic* to travel up to 26 miles per hour (42 kph).

To keep the boilers hot enough to make steam, the *Titanic* carried a small mountain of coal—almost 8,000 tons (7,257 mt) worth!

Titanic's huge engines were located in the bottom of the ship.

A scene from a movie about the *Titanic* that shows men shoveling coal into the ship's boilers

Stopping a 53,000-ton (48,080 mt) ship traveling at full speed would also take a lot of strength. The *Titanic* had five different **anchors**, including a center anchor that was the largest ever made. At nearly 16 tons (14 mt), it took around 20 Clydesdale horses to move it!

A replica, or copy, of *Titanic*'s huge center anchor

HINGLEY. NETHERTON.

HINGLEY SOLE MAKERS

DUDLEY

HALLS LATEST PATENT

Clydesdales are strong, muscular horses.

A Floating Palace

The *Titanic* would offer more than just a fast way to cross the ocean. For first-class passengers, it was like traveling in a **palace**. The ship had a swimming pool, a gym, libraries, and fancy restaurants. Its grand staircase was lit by a curved glass **skylight**. The *Titanic* even had a spa for its wealthiest guests.

What the *Titanic*'s grand staircase might have looked like

There were 350 rooms and four ultra-luxurious parlor **suites** for first-class passengers. Each parlor suite had up to five separate rooms and was decorated with fine art and furniture. However, life on the *Titanic* was very different for those passengers in third class, where four people shared a single room. In addition, there were only two bathtubs for all 710 steerage passengers! Still, the accommodations for even for the poorest guests on the *Titanic* were considered very comfortable.

At the time, the most expensive ticket on the *Titanic* cost $4,350. That's about $70,000 in today's money!

This is what a first-class suite on the *Titanic* might have looked like.

Third-class passengers slept in rooms much like this one. Each one had running water—a luxury at the time.

NEW TECHNOLOGY

The White Star Line designed the *Titanic* to include all the best and newest **technology**. In the early 1900s, very few buildings in the United States had elevators. The *Titanic* had three. Many travelers had never seen electric lights, yet the *Titanic* shined with more than 10,000 of them.

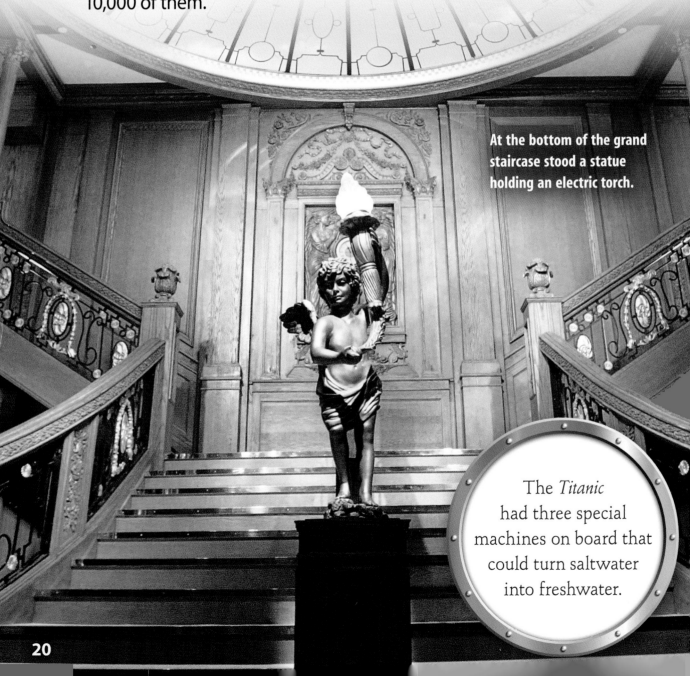

At the bottom of the grand staircase stood a statue holding an electric torch.

The *Titanic* had three special machines on board that could turn saltwater into freshwater.

The ship's communication system was also the most advanced in the world. There were 50 telephones on board that the crew and first-class passengers could use to talk to one another. In addition, smaller ships could send **telegraph** messages up to only 100 miles (160 km). The *Titanic* could send telegrams up to 2,000 miles (3,219 km)! One couple, Isidor and Ida Straus, used telegrams every day to communicate with their son who was on a different ship!

A model of *Titanic*'s radio room, where people could send messages

Isidor and Ida Straus

SAFETY FIRST?

The *Titanic* was built for safety, as well. Sixteen huge watertight compartments were spread along the hull of the ship. Thick walls called bulkheads separated these rooms. The purpose of the compartments was to trap water in case the ship collided with something and started leaking. Many people believed these safety features made the ship unsinkable.

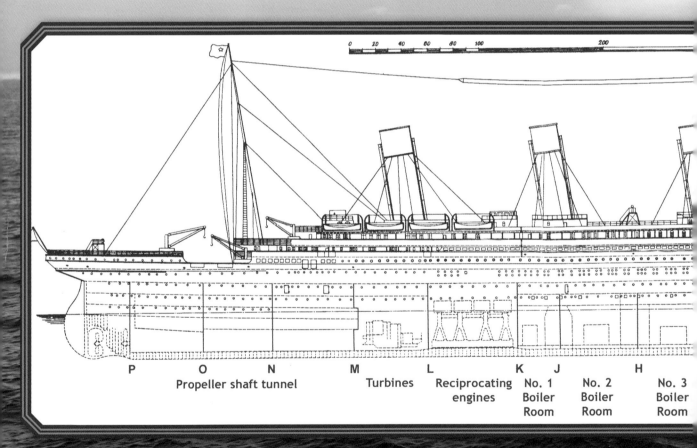

The 16 bulkheads are shown in red on this diagram. The ship would still be able to stay afloat even if the first four compartments filled with water.

Thomas Andrews's original plan included bulkheads that stretched almost to the top of the ship. That design would have made the ship even safer. However, the **executives** at the White Star Line didn't like that idea because the taller bulkheads would take away space from the first-class dining hall. The executives ordered Andrews to change the design so the bulkheads went up only a few floors. Unfortunately, if ocean water flooded above the bulkheads, they would be useless.

Special doors connected the sixteen watertight rooms. The *Titanic*'s captain could close these doors if the ship hit something.

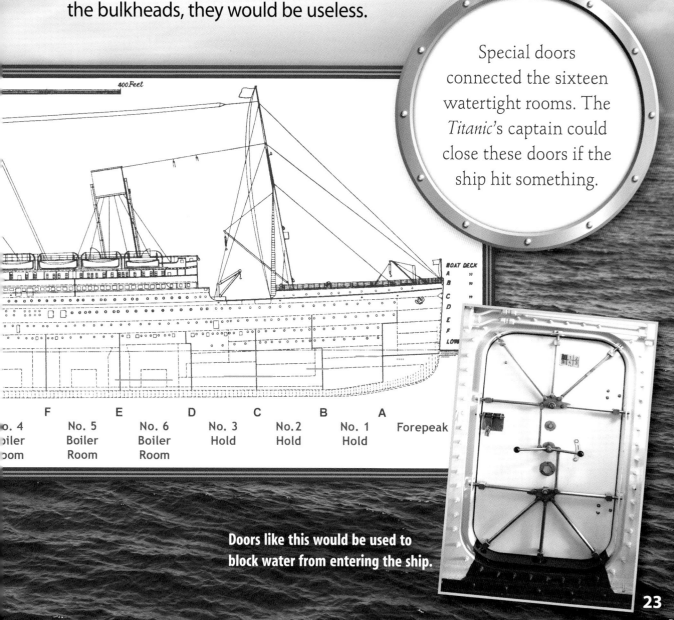

400 Feet

BOAT DECK
A
B
C
D
E
F
LOW

F	E	D	C	B	A	
o. 4 ꞵiler ꞵom	No. 5 Boiler Room	No. 6 Boiler Room	No. 3 Hold	No. 2 Hold	No. 1 Hold	Forepeak

Doors like this would be used to block water from entering the ship.

LACK OF LIFEBOATS

In the unlikely event of a disaster, the ship would need lifeboats to transport its crew and passengers to safety. The *Titanic* was large enough to carry 3,500 people—nearly the size of a small town. The original plan for the huge ship included 64 lifeboats, which could hold 4,000 people.

The law at the time required the largest ships to carry only 16 lifeboats. However, there had never been a ship as big as the *Titanic*.

There were 3,560 life vests on board.

Lifeboats from the *Titanic*

Ismay and other executives at the White Star Line did not like this plan. They worried that so many lifeboats would **clutter** the first-class passenger deck and block the view of the ocean. The company agreed to carry 20 lifeboats. However, this meant there would be room for only 1,200 people. General manager Alexander Carlisle was outraged. He believed cutting the number of lifeboats was a terrible mistake. Carlisle ended up quitting his job over the disagreement.

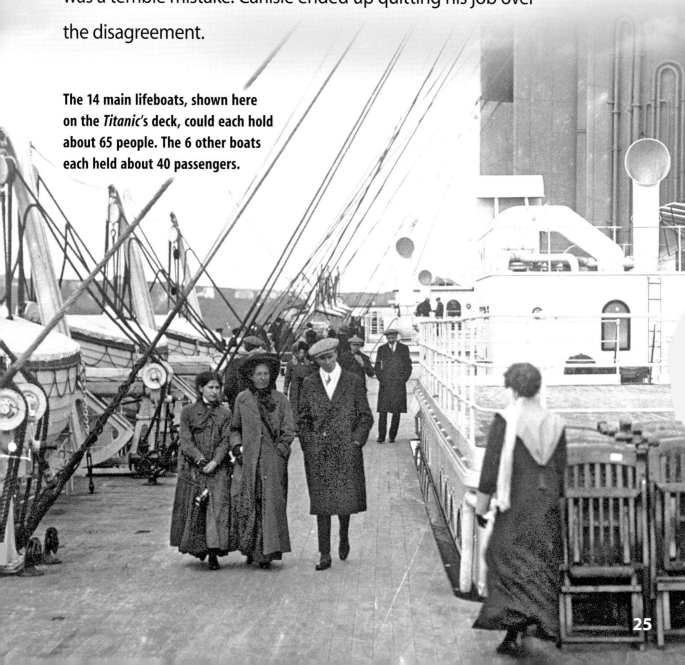

The 14 main lifeboats, shown here on the *Titanic*'s deck, could each hold about 65 people. The 6 other boats each held about 40 passengers.

SETTING SAIL

After three busy years of construction, the *Titanic* was finally completed on March 31, 1912. In the year after it first slid into the water in Belfast, workers had carefully put the finishing touches on the massive ship. All that was left were the **sea trials**. They would determine whether the *Titanic* could properly turn and stop, and whether it had been built well enough to safely cross the Atlantic Ocean to America.

It took four tugboats to pull the *Titanic* from its berth into the ocean.

What the finished Titanic might have looked like sailing out into the open sea

At 6:00 AM on April 2, 1912, the time had come to put the *Titanic* to the test. Captain Edward John Smith ordered all engines on full speed, and the **hulking** ship sprang to life. He put the ship through tests for turning, sailing, and stopping. The sea trials were a complete success. The *Titanic* was ready for her **maiden voyage** as thousands of excited passengers waited eagerly to step on board the ship of dreams.

The *Titanic* was scheduled to sail on April 10, 1912.

THE SHIP OF DREAMS

The *Titanic* was the most luxurious steamship of its time—and, perhaps, of any time. What amenities did first-class passengers enjoy?

The wealthiest passengers could eat in a private restaurant. Tables were set with porcelain plates and cups. The menu included duck, salmon, and beef.

A first-class lounge was decorated to look like a palace. It had elegant furniture and a marble fireplace.

Beautiful objects, such as this gold-covered lead grill, decorated the areas used by first-class passengers.

Wealthy passengers could take a dip in a heated swimming pool and then relax in a Turkish-style spa.

The luxury dining hall could seat hundreds of passengers. Musicians entertained the guests with classical music.

GLOSSARY

amenities (uh-MEN-i-teez) features that provide comfort

anchors (ANG-kerz) heavy objects lowered from a ship that help hold the ship in place

architect (AHR-ki-tekt) a person who designs buildings or ships and manages their construction

berth (BURTH) the place reserved for a ship at a shipyard or dock

boilers (BOI-luhrs) tanks in which water is heated to make steam

clutter (KLUHT-UR) to crowd

executives (eg-ZEK-yuh-tivz) people who help run a company

hulking (HUHL-king) giant and heavy

hull (HUHL) the frame or body of a ship

immigrants (IM-uh-gruhntz) people who come from one country to live permanently in a new one

inlet (IN-let) a narrow body of water running from a larger body of water

keel (KEEL) the bottom of a ship's hull, or frame

luxurious (luhk-ZHUH-ree-uhss) fancy and comfortable

maiden voyage (MEY-den VOI-ij) the first trip of a ship

majestic (muh-JES-tik) grand and beautiful

mansion (MAN-shuhn) a large and grand house

massive (MASS-iv) very large

ocean liner (OH-shun LIE-nuhr) a passenger ship that transports people across the ocean

palace (PAL-iss) the grand home of a king or queen

passengers (PASS-uhn-jurz) people who travel on a boat or a vehicle

plates (PLAITS) thin, flat sheets of metal

rival (RYE-vuhl) a person or thing that competes against another person or thing

riveters (RIV-it-urs) people whose job it is to use pins to attach metal to other pieces of metal

sea trials (SEE TRY-uls) tests given to a ship before allowing it to carry passengers

shipyard (SHIP-yahrd) a place where ships are constructed

skylight (SKY-lite) a window in a roof or ceiling

slipways (SLIP-weyz) areas in shipyards where ships are built or repaired

steerage (STEER-ij) the place on a ship, usually at the bottom, where passengers with the least expensive tickets stay

suites (SWEETS) connected series of rooms

technology (tek-NOL-uh-jee) the use of science and engineering to solve problems

telegraph (TEL-uh-graf) a machine for sending messages over long distances using a code of electric signals

BIBLIOGRAPHY

Brewster, Hugh, and Laurie Coulter. *882 1/2 Amazing Answers to Your Questions About the Titanic.* New York: Scholastic (1999).

Charles River Editors. *Building the RMS Titanic: The Construction of the World's Most Famous Ship.* New York: CreateSpace (2014).

Green, Rod. *Building the Titanic: An Epic Tale of the Creation of History's Most Famous Ocean Liner.* New York: Reader's Digest (2011).

READ MORE

Blake, Kevin. *Titanic's Fatal Voyage (Titanica).* New York: Bearport (2018).

Giannini, Alex. *Titanic's Passengers and Crew (Titanica).* New York: Bearport (2018).

Goldish, Meish. *Discovering Titanic's Remains (Titanica).* New York: Bearport (2018).

LEARN MORE ONLINE

To learn more about creating the *Titanic*, visit
www.bearportpublishing.com/Titanica

INDEX

ABOUT THE AUTHOR

Kevin Blake lives in Providence, Rhode Island, with his wife, Melissa, his son, Sam, and his daughter, Ilana. He has written more than 20 books for young readers.

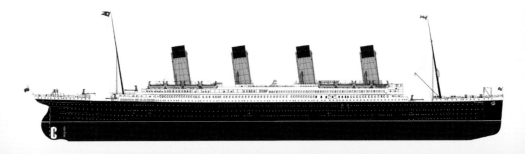